I0099495

# The Law of Financial Success

# The Law of Financial Success
## by Edward E Beals

Start Publishing PD LLC
Copyright © 2024 by Start Publishing PD LLC

All rights reserved, including the right to reproduce this book or portions thereof in any form whatsoever.

Start Publishing PD is a registered trademark of Start Publishing PD LLC
Manufactured in the United States of America

Cover art: Shutterstock/Taisiya Kozorez

Cover design: Jennifer Do

10  9  8  7  6  5  4  3  2  1

ISBN 979-8-8809-1726-6

# Table of Contents

# Introduction

"The Law of Financial Success!" To some this title may appear presumptuous, and indicative of an overweening vanity on the part of a writer who wishes to impress upon the world the belief that his ideas and opinions regarding the subject of Financial Success are of such transcendent value as to be worthy of the appellation of The *Law*. Patience, patience, good friends, the author has no such bumptious conceit—no such vainglory. He is not attempting to frame a law; not seeking to impose upon the world a set code of conduct, emanating from his finite mind, and claiming for it the authority of a *Law*. Nay, nay, he has learned to smile at such exhibitions of folly on the part of some so-called thinkers of our times, and begs to be absolved from the suspicion of such childish desire or intent.

He does not wish to pose as the formulator, discoverer, or enunciator of a new Law. He knows that any Law, to be really a LAW, must rest upon the eternal foundations of Reality, and cannot be created, made, or formed by the finite mind of man. And, so, good friends, he does not claim to have made, created or formed this great Universal Law to the consideration of which this little book is devoted. It is not his mental offspring, but a great, eternal, universal Law of Life, which springs from the source of all Laws of Life. In fact, it is an integral part and portion of the *One Great Law* underlying all Life, and fits into those other Natural Laws, which, when combined in an Universal Harmony, form the outward manifestation of the *Great Law* underlying, inherent in, and manifesting in all that we call Life.

"But," you may ask, "is there then really a fundamental *Law* underlying that which we call Financial Success? Is there a *Law* which if once discovered, understood and practiced, will enable one to accomplish that for which this great modern world is so strenuously striving, toiling and desiring? Is there a *Law*, which, when operated will make one the master of Financial Success, instead of a mere blind groper after its fruits? Is, indeed, Financial Success the result of the operations of a *Law*, instead of the operation of mere luck, chance, or accident?"

Ah, yea, good friends, all this that you seek comes only from the application and operation of a great *Law*, which the successful men and women of the world make use of either consciously or unconsciously. And this great *Law* is as well defined as is any other Natural Law, and when grasped and understood may be practiced and operated just as may any of its related Laws on other planes of universal activity. There is no such thing in Nature as blind chance, accident, or uncaused lack. Everything in Nature operates in accordance with *Law*. *Law* underlies everything. You may doubt this, but stop a moment and try to think of anything in our finite world that is not the effect of some cause. A great stone is dislodged and rolls down the mountain side, striking a tree which it uproots and sends rolling down into a stream which is dammed up, causing a flood that sweeps away a fertile field, and so on, and on, effect succeeding effect. Was all this mere blind chance? Not at all. The stone was dislodged in response to the operation of causes that had been at work for centuries disintegrating the stone, and which caused the boulder to become dislodged exactly at the moment when the inherent power of the Cause reached that particular stage. There was no more chance in the dislodgment of the stone than there was in the striking of a clock that had been wound up a day, or a week, or a year before. It was all the result of invariable and consistent *Law*. And so was the direction of the stone's fall; and all the succeeding incidents.

But mark you this, had some Man been able to discover and understand the *Law* in operation in that latent power inherent in the stone, he would have been able to prevent the stone striking the tree and causing all the resulting damage; and he might, and would have been able to divert the stone from its path of damage, and turn it into some place in which it would have done no harm, and in which he could have broken it into bits at his leisure, and thus secured building stone for the foundation of his cottage, or the material from which a hard roadbed could have been made. The *Law* behind the stone was always there, and was consistent in its operation, and yet Man, by the power of his mind could have turned the *Law* into his own channels and converted it to his use. He could have made a servant and a slave of this Universal Law, instead of allowing it to master him, and become his tyrant; for in this way has man mastered the forces of Gravitation Steam, Hydraulics and Electricity, which once mastered him.

Thus has Man risen from savagery and barbarism into what he is today. And thus will he advance from what he is today into what he will become in the days to come—a creature as much superior to Man of today as the latter is superior to the barbarian. The story of Man's Attainment may be expressed in these words: "The subjugation and mastery of Nature's forces," And so it will ever be. Man first is mastered and operated upon by Nature's forces. Then he discovers the *Law* underlying these forces. Then he harnesses the force, and makes it work his will. As the great English scientist Ray Lankester has recently declared in his works: "Man is held to be a part of Nature, a product of the definite and orderly evolution which is universal; a being resulting from and driven by the one great nexus of mechanism which we call

Nature. He stands alone, face to face with the relentless mechanism. It if his destiny to understand and control it."

"But," you may object, "this is all very well, and undoubtedly true of the physical forces of Nature, but financial Success cannot be classed with these forces. Why, it is purely a latter-day development, and cannot be identified with the great Natural forces of which you have spoken."

Patience, again, good friends! As we proceed you shall see that the Law of Financial Success is a part and parcel of the Great Law of Use and Nourishment which is in operation all through animal and vegetable life. It is the same *Law* that manifests in the form of the securing of food by the animal, the securing of nourishment by the plant. Nay, more, it is the same *Law* by and through which Nature operates when it causes the atom of oxygen to attract to itself the two atoms of hydrogen in order to form the molecule of water. Water all over the world is composed of just these two substances, combined in just this proportion. The atom of oxygen has the power to operate the great Law of Attraction and Use, upon the two atoms of hydrogen, and when it draws them to itself, the tiny globule of water results.

The oxygen needs the hydrogen to accomplish its life mission; the plant needs the drop of water to accomplish its life mission; and the animal needs the plant to accomplish its life mission. And modern man needs Financial Success to accomplish his life's mission. And each one draws to itself that which it needs in proportion to its use of the *Law*. The same *Law* in its various forms is in operation everywhere in the same way.

But in the chemical, mineral, vegetable and animal worlds, the desire which prompts the attraction, and the will which manifests the desire, are unconsciously exerted. With man, it is different, he has developed consciousness, and to live his full life, and to accomplish his manifest destiny he must use that consciousness in discovering, understanding and availing himself of the natural forces inherent in the *Law*.

And this is why this little book has been written—to point out; first the existence of the Law of Financial Success; second, to lead you to an understanding of it; and third, to give you the result of the experience of successful men in the direction of operating the *Law*. And now, to "sum up" this introduction, as our legal friends would say, the writer asks you to consider the following propositions:

All progress, whether physical, mental, moral, spiritual or financial, is based upon *Law*. And he who wins success in any line does so because he has followed the *Law* or *Law*S pertaining to his business, whether he does it consciously or unconsciously.

Some of our great "Captains of Industry," who have won marvelous successes in financial affairs (though they may have failed as moral or spiritual beings), have won their great success along this line because they, consciously or unconsciously, have discovered the underlying *Law*, and by concentrating upon it alone, to the exclusion of everything else in life, have manifested the operation of the *Law* to an almost abnormal degree.

What most of us want is "all 'round" success, but what we must remember is that no one can be an "all 'round" success without Financial Independence. No matter how much good a person may want to do, he is handicapped by a lack of money. All the air-castles that he has built; all the beautiful plans that he has created: all the cherished desires to do good—all go unfulfilled because there is no money with which to complete them. Before these air-castles can become real buildings; before these plans can become realities; before these great desires can be fulfilled; before any of these great things can be manifested into living realities—the *Law* must be seen, understood, and put into conscious operation. And the purpose of this little book is to tell you *How to Do It!*

For several years the writer has seen the need, among advanced thought circles, of a book filling this want. In his own life he has found that Financial Success is not a matter of grind, and rush, and fight and struggle. It is a matter of getting into harmony with the *Law*, and then following that *Law* to its logical conclusion. In this little book he will place this information and the result of his experience. In it he will state the *Law*—how to get in harmony with it—and what to do to keep in the closest touch with it.

This book is no magic potion to be swallowed with wonderful results—it is, instead, a plain statement of the *Law*, so that all who run may read, and then act. And he who acts will win success, because he is following the *Law* that has been laid down from time immemorial. Whether rich or poor, successful or unsuccessful—it matters not— this book will be of great value to you. If you are a natural money-maker, you must have been using this *Law* unconsciously, and in such case this book will enable you to do consciously that which you have been partly doing unconsciously. If you are unsuccessful, and money seems not to be attracted by or to you, this book will guide your thought and actions into proper channels where you will be able to manifest the *Law* and thus get the highest possible results.

And, now that you have been told of the feast of good things ahead of you, draw up your chair to the table and partake of what nourishing food has been provided in the following pages. After all, you know, "the proof of the pudding lies in the eating thereof," and so fall to and taste that which has been gathered together for your mental, physical and financial well-being. And now, while you are filling your plates, the writer proposes the opening toast, to be drunk in Nature's sparkling fluid: "Here's to you—may you live long and prosper by following the Law of Financial Success!"

# Money

There is no idea that seems so much misunderstood as this idea of "Money." On the one hand we find many people engaged in a mad chase after "money for moneys sake," and on the other hand, many others who are decrying money as the root of all evil, and severely criticizing the tendency of the age to seek money actively. Both of these classes of people are wrong—they are occupying the opposite sides of the road of reason, whereas truth is found here, as always, "in the middle of the road."

The man who seeks money at a thing of value in itself—the man who worships money at a very god— such a man is a fool, for he is mistaking the symbol for the reality. And, likewise, the man who decries the pursuit and desire for money as a foul, evil thing—he who would make of money a devil—this man is likewise a fool. The wise man is he who sees money as a symbol of something else behind, and who is not deluded by mistaking the shadow for the substance, either for good or evil. The wise man makes neither a god nor a devil of money—he sees it as a symbol of almost everything that man may obtain from the outside world, and he respects it as such. He sees, while it is true that avarice and greed are detestable and hurtful qualities of mind, still the lack of the proper desire for, and striving after money, makes of man a creature devoid of all that makes life worth the living.

When the sane man desires money, he really desires the many things that money will purchase. Money is the symbol of nearly everything that is necessary for man's wellbeing and happiness. With it he opens the door to all sorts of opportunities, and without it he can accomplish practically nothing, Money is the tool with which man may carve many beautiful things, and without the aid of which he is helpless. Money is but the concentrated essence of things desired, created and established by society in its present stage of development. There have been times in which there was no money—there may be times coming in which the race will have passed beyond the need of money as the symbol of exchange and possession—but, be this as it may, the fact remains that now, right here in the beginning of the Twentieth Century, there in nothing that is so necessary for man's well-being and content as this much-abused money.

Remember this, first, last and all the tune, that when I say, "man needs money," I mean that he needs the many things that money will purchase for him. And for one to decry the desire for money is for him to decry the desire for nearly all the good and desirable things of life. As a recent writer has said: "Unless a man acquires money, then shall he not eat; nor be clothed; nor have shelter; nor books; nor music; nor anything else that makes life worth living for one who thinks and feels."

The people who decry the desire for money are generally those who have found themselves lacking in the qualities that tend to attract money; or else those who are in possession of money that has been inherited, or is otherwise acquired without the labor, excitement or satisfaction of having been made by themselves. With the first mentioned class it is a case of "sour grapes"; with the second it is financial dyspepsia, which has left the victim devoid of a normal appetite.

In spite of the loud cries and protests of our long-haired brothers and short-haired sisters—so-called "reformers"—money is still necessary in order that man may have the necessities of life, as well as a few luxuries. We cannot live on beautiful theories, but must have bread and batter, and potatoes, and sometimes a piece of cake or pie— and it takes money to get them. Money means freedom, independence, liberty, and the ability to do great good, as well as great evil. It means the opportunity to carry out great plant and to fulfill great ideals. It means the filling in of those mental pictures that we have sketched out in our minds. It means the chance of materializing those airy "Castles in Spain" that we have dwelt upon in moments of hopeful ecstasy. Ah, yes, money is the wizard, able and willing to work wonders. It is, indeed, the genie who can and will do its master's bidding.

I hold that in the present stage of evolution of man, money is to mankind what air, water, sunshine and mother-earth are to the plant—it is nourishment. And, as in the plant, the desire for nourishment is a natural and worthy instinct, so is the desire for this financial nourishment in man a perfectly natural and worthy instinct—it is the working of the same natural law. And, mark you this, that as the desire of the plant is a natural indication of the existence of the nourishment-need, so is this desire in the breast of man a certain indication of the possibility of its satisfaction and attainment, if natural laws are but followed. Nature is no mocker—it causes no desire to spring up in a living thing, unless it also endows that living thing with the faculties and powers to attain that which it craves. A realization of this great natural law will do many of my readers much good just now.

But note this, also, nature does not encourage the hoarding up of anything for the mere sake of acquisition. It punishes this error severely. The Law of Use underlies all of nature's instinctive cravings. It desires that the living thing shall draw to itself the nourishment and material it needs, in order to use it. And this desire for money on the part of man is governed by this same law—the Law of Use. Nature wishes you to desire money—to attract it to you—to possess and acquire it—and lastly, and most important of all, to use it. By using money, and keeping it working and in action, you will fall in line with the workings of this great Law of Use. By falling in with this Law, you work in harmony with the great natural forces and purposes. You bring yourself into harmony with the Cosmic Plan, instead of opposing it, and when man so brings himself into harmony with the natural forces around him, he reduces friction and receives the reward that comes to all living things that work with, instead of against, the *Law*.

So, friends, in closing this chapter, I would say to you: Be not afraid, but assert the desirability of the possession and use of money: recognize that it is your natural right to possess it, just as it is the natural right of the plant to sunshine, light and air. And do more than this—it belongs to you—demand it of the *Law*, just as does the plant.

Cease all this talk of the beauty of poverty, and the joy of the humble—you know that in the bottom of your heart you do not mean a word of it You know that you are just saying these things because you are afraid that you cannot have that which you want. Throw off this mask of hypocrisy, and self-deception, and stand out in the open like a man, throwing your head up and looking the world in the face, saying, "Yes, I do desire Money; I want it and I want it earnestly, and through the *Law* I demand it as my rightful inheritance—and I'm going to get it, beginning right now!"

Throw off the shackles of the slave, and assert your freedom. Assert your own mastery of that which is your own. Don't be afraid to assert what you want, and to see it clearly ahead of you—then march straight onward to the mark, without turning to the right, or to the left, without fear or favor, without flinching or fouling—straight to the mark which is called Financial Success! For in that goal, alone, may you find that for which you seek—that which your heart desires.

# Mental Attitude

You remember the saying of the sacred writer: "As a man thinketh in his heart, so is he." A truer statement never was uttered. For every man or woman is what he or she is, by reason of what he or she has thought. We have thought ourselves into what we are. One's place in life is largely determined by his Mental Attitude.

Mental Attitude is the result of the current of one's thoughts, ideas, ideals, feelings, and beliefs. You are constantly at work building up a Mental Attitude, which is not only making your character but which is also having its influence upon the outside world, both in the direction of your effect upon other people, as well as your quality of attracting toward yourself that which is in harmony with the prevailing mental state held by you. Is it not most important, then, that this building should be done with the best possible materials—according to the best plan—with the best tools?

The keynote of this chapter is: "A positive Mental Attitude Wins Financial Success." Before going any further, let us define the word "Positive" and its opposite, "Negative," and then see how the former wins success and the latter attracts failure. In the sense in which I use the terms, "Positive" means Confident Expectation, Self-Confidence, Courage, Initiative, Energy, Optimism, Expectation of Good, not Evil— of Wealth, not Poverty—Belief in Oneself and in the *Law*, etc., etc.; "Negative" means Fear, Worry, Expectation of Undesirable Things, Lack of Confidence in Oneself and the *Law*, etc., etc.

In the first place Mental Attitude tends towards success by its power in the direction of "making us over" into individuals possessing qualities conducive to success. Many people go through the world bemoaning their lack of the faculties, qualities or temperament that they instinctively recognize an active factors in the attainment of success. They see others possessing these desirable qualities moving steadily forward to their goal, and they also feel if they themselves were but possessed of these same qualities they, too, might attain the same desirable results. Now, so far, their reasoning is all right—but they do not go far enough. They fail here because they imagine that since they have not the desired qualities at the moment, they can never expect to possess them. They regard their minds as something that once fixed and built can never be improved upon, repaired, rebuilt, or enlarged. Right here is where the majority of people "fall down," to use the expressive although slangy words of the day.

As a matter of fact, the great scientific authorities of the present time distinctly teach that a man by diligent care and practice, may completely change his character, temperament, and habits. He may kill out undesirable traits of character, and replace them by new and desirable traits, qualities and faculties. The brain is now known to be but the instrument and tool of something called Mind, which uses the brain as its instrument of expression.

And the brain is also now known to be composed of millions of tiny cells, the majority of which are not in use. It is also known that if one turns his attention and interest in certain directions, the unused cells in the area of his brain which is the center of such subject, will be stimulated into action and will begin to manifest actively. Not only this, but the stimulated sections of cells will begin also to actively manifest their reproductive qualities, and new brain cells will be evolved, grown and developed in order to furnish proper mental tools with which to manifest the new desires, qualities and feelings pressing forward for expression.

Scientific Character Building is not a mere idle theory, but a live, vital, actual, practical fact, being put into operation in the psychological laboratories of the country, and by thousands of private individuals all over the world who are rapidly "making themselves over" by this method. And the prevailing Mental Attitude is the pattern upon which the brain cells build. If you can but grasp this truth you have the key to success in your hands.

Now, let us consider the second phase of the action of Mental Attitude toward Financial Success. I allude to the effect upon others of one's Mental Attitude. Did you ever stop long enough to think that we are constantly giving other people suggestive impressions of ourselves and qualities? Do you not know that, if you go about with the Mental Attitude of Discouragement, Fear, Lack of Self-Confidence, and all the other Negative qualities of mind, other people are sure to catch the impression and govern themselves toward you accordingly?

Let a man come into your presence for the purpose of doing business with you and if he lack confidence in himself and in the things he wishes to sell you, you will at once catch his spirit and will feel that you have no confidence in him or the things he if offering. You will catch his mental atmosphere at once, and he will suffer thereby. But let this same man fill himself up with thoughts, feelings, and ideals of Enthusiasm, Success, Self-Confidence, Confidence in his proposition, etc., and he will fairly radiate success toward you, and you will unconsciously "take stock" in him and interest in his goods, and the chances are that you will be willing and glad to do business with him.

Do you not know men who radiate Failure, Discouragement and "I Can't"? Are you not affected by their manifested Mental Attitude to their hurt? And, on the other hand, do you not know men who are so filled with Confidence, Courage, Enthusiasm, Fearlessness, and Energy, that the moment you come into their presence, or they into yours, you at once catch their spirit, and respond thereto? I contend that there is an actual atmosphere surrounding each of these men—which if you are sensitive enough you can feel—one of repulsion, and the other of attraction. And further, that these atmospheres are the result of the constant daily thought of these men or the Mental Attitude of each toward life. Think over this a bit, and you will see at once just how the *Law* works.

The third phase of the action of Mental Attitude towards Financial Success may be called the working of the Law of Attraction. Now, without Attempting to advance any wild theories, I still most assert that all thinking, observing men have noticed the operation of a mental Law of Attraction, whereby "like attracts like."

Avoiding all theories on the subject, I state the general principle that a man's Mental Attitude acts a magnet, attracting to him the things, objects, circumstances, environments, and people in harmony with that Mental Attitude. If we think Success firmly and hold it properly before as, it tends to build up a constant Mental Attitude which invariably attracts to us the things conducive to its attainment and materialization. If we hold the ideal of Financial Success—in short, Money—our Mental Attitude will gradually form and crystallize the *money* ideal. And the things pertaining to Money—people calculated to help us win Money—circumstances tending to bring us Money—opportunities for making Money—in fact, all sorts of Money-things—will be attracted toward us.

You think this visionary talk, do you? Well, then, just make a careful study of any man who has attained Financial Success and see whether or not his prevailing attitude is not that of expectation of money. He holds the Mental Attitude as an ideal, and he is constantly realizing that ideal.

Fix your mind firmly upon anything, good or bad in the world, and you attract it to you or are attracted to it in obedience to the *Law*. You attract to you the things you expect, think about and hold in your Mental Attitude.

This is no superstitious idea, but a firmly established, scientific, psychological fact.

To further illustrate the workings of the above *Law*, "like attracts like," and "birds of a feather flock together," I might here present the theory which of late has been the subject of much discussion among noted psychologists, i.e., that there are thought currents in the mental realm just as there are air currents in the atmosphere, and ocean currents in the seas. For instance, there are thought currents of vice and others of virtue; thought currents of fear and others of courage; thought currents of hate and others of love; thought currents of poverty and others of wealth. And, further than this, the person who thinks and talks and expects poverty is drawn into the poverty thought currents of the world and attracts to himself others who think and talk along the same lines; and vice versa: the person who thinks, talks and expects wealth and prosperity attracts, or is attracted to, people of wealth and comes, in time, to share their prosperity with them. I am not trying to champion this theory, but if it should be true it behooves each one of us to watch our thought and talk, getting rid of the poverty thought, and in its place substituting the wealth and prosperity thought.

Sweep out from the chambers of your mind all these miserable negative thoughts like "I can't," "That's just my luck," "I knew I'd do it," "Poor me," etc., and then fill up the mind with the positive, invigorating, helpful, forceful, compelling ideals of Success, Confidence, and expectation of that which you desire; and just as the steel filings fly to the attraction of the magnet, so will that which you need fly to you in response to this great natural principle of mental action—the Law of Attraction. Begin this very moment and build up a new ideal—that of Financial Success—see it mentally— expect it—demand it! This is the way to create it in your Mental Attitude.

# Fear and Worry

The great negative note in the lives of most people is Fear. Fear is the mother of all the negative emotions, and her brood is found clustering very closely around her. Worry, Lack of Confidence, Bashfulness, Irresolution, Timidity, Depression, and all the rest of the negative brood of feelings and emotions are the progeny of Fear. Without Fear none of these minor emotions or feelings would exist. By killing off the parent of this possible brood of mental vampires, you escape the entire coming generations of negative thoughts, and thus keep your Mental Attitude garden free from these pests and nuisances.

Fear and the emotions that come from its being do more to paralyze useful effort, good work, and finely thought-out plans, than aught else known to man. It is the great hobgoblin of the race. It has ruined the lives of thousands of people. It has destroyed the finely budding characters of men and women, and made negative individuals of them in the place of strong, reliant, courageous doers of useful things.

Worry is the oldest child of Fear. It settles down upon one's mind, and crowds out all of the developing good things to be found there. Like the cuckoo in the sparrow's nest, it destroys the rightful occupants of the mind. Laid there as an egg by its parent, Fear, Worry soon hatches out and begins to make trouble. In place of the cheerful and positive "I Can and I Will" harmony, Worry begins to rasp out in raucous tones: "Supposin'," "What if," "But," "I can't," "I'm unlucky," "I never could do things right," "Things never turn oat right with me" and so on until all the minor notes have been sounded. It makes one sick bodily, and inert mentally. It retards one's program, and is a constant stumbling block in our path upward.

The worst thing about Fear and Worry is that while they exhaust a great part of the energy of the average person, they give nothing good in return. Nobody ever accomplished a single thing by reason of Fear and Worry. Fear and Worry never helped one along a single inch on the road to Success. And they never will, because their whole tendency is to retard progress, and not to advance it. The majority of things that we fear and worry about never come to pass at all, and the few that do actually materialize are never as bad as we feared they would be. It is not the cares, trials and troubles of today that unnerve us and break us down—it is the troubles that we fear may come sometime in the future. Everyone is able to bear the burdens of today, but when he heaps on the burdens of tomorrow, the next day, and the day after that, he is doing his mind an injustice, and it is no wonder that after a bit he heaps on the last straw that breaks the back of the mental camel.

The energy, work, activity and thought that we expend on these imaginary "maybe" troubles of the future would enable us to master and conquer the troubles of each day as they arise. Nature gives each of us a reserve supply of strength and energy upon which to draw and oppose unexpected troubles and problems as they come upon us each day. But we poor, silly mortals draw upon this reserve force and dissipate it in combating the imaginary troubles of next week or next year, the majority of which never really put in an appearance—and when we have need of the force to oppose some real trouble of the day we find ourselves bankrupt of power and energy, and are apt to go down in defeat, or else be compelled to beat an inglorious retreat.

I tell you, friends, that if you once learn the secret of killing off this vampire of Fear, and thus prevent the rearing of her hateful brood of reptile emotions, life will seem a different thing to you. You will begin to realize what it is to live. You will learn what it is to have a mind cleared of weeds, and fresh to grow healthy thoughts, feelings, emotions and ambitions.

And you will find that with Fear killed out, you will cease to give out to others the suggestions of incompetence, lack of reliance on yourself, and the other impressions that hurt one's chances. You will find that when you are rid of Fear you will radiate hope, and confidence, and ability, and will impress all those with whom you come in contact.

And you will find also that the eradication of Fear will work wonders in your Mental Attitude, and the operation of it through the Law of Attraction. When one fears a thing he really attracts it to him, just as if he desired it. The reason is this—when one desires or fears a thing (in either case the principle is the same) he creates a mental picture of the thing, which mental picture has a tendency toward materialization. With this mental picture in his mind—if beholds to it long enough—he draws the things or conditions to him, and thus "thought takes form in action and being." The majority of our fears and worries are silly little things that take our thought for a moment, and then are gone. They are great wasters of energy, but we do not concentrate on any one of them long enough to put into operation the Law of Attraction.

And so you see, that unless you get rid of Fear, it will tend to draw toward you the thing you fear, or else force you toward the thing itself. Fear makes of the feared object a name around which you circle and flutter, like the moth, until at last you make plunge right into the heat of the flame and are consumed. Kill out Fear, by all means.

"But how may I kill it out?" you cry. Very easily! This is the method: Suppose you had a roomful of darkness. Would you start to shovel or sweep out the darkness? Or would you not throw open the window and admit the light? When the light pours in, the darkness disappears. And so with the darkness of Fear—throw open the windows, and "let a little sunshine in." Let the thoughts, feelings, and ideals of Courage, Confidence and Fearlessness poor into your mind, and Fear will vanish. Whenever Fear shows itself in your mind, administer the antidote of Fearlessness immediately.

Say to yourself: "I am Fearless; I Fear Nothing; I am Courageous," Let the sunshine pour in.

# Faith

Faith is a word that has been often misused, misapplied and misunderstood. To many it means simply that attitude of mind which will accept anything that is told it, merely because someone else has said it—credulity, in fact. But those who have penetrated within the shell of the word know that it means something far more real than this—something imbedded deep down in the Heart of Things. To those who understand the *Law*, Faith is the trolley-pole which one raises to meet the Great Forces of Life and Nature, and by means of which one receives the inflow of the Power which is behind, and in all things, and is enabled to apply that Power to the running of his own affairs.

To some, it may seem a far cry from Faith to Financial Success, but to those who have demonstrated the truths enunciated in this little book, the two are closely interwoven. For one to attain Financial Success he must first have Faith in Himself; second, Faith in his Fellowman; and third, Faith in the *Law*.

Faith in oneself is of primary importance, for unless one has it he can never accomplish anything; can never influence any other person's opinion of him; can never attract to himself the things, persons and circumstances necessary for his welfare. A man must first learn to believe in himself before he will be able to make others believe in him. People are prone to take a person at his own estimate. If one is weak, negative and lacking in self-confidence, he surrounds himself with an atmosphere of negativity which unfavorably impresses those with whom he comes in contact. If one be strong, confident and positive, he radiates like qualities, and those coming in contact with him receive an impression of these qualities. The world believes in those who believe in themselves. And so you see it is of the utmost importance to you that you cultivate this Faith in yourself.

And not only does Faith in yourself operate in the direction of influencing others with whom you come in contact, but it also has a most positive bearing upon your own mental statue and thoughts. If you deaden your mind with a negative attitude toward yourself, you stifle budding ideas, thoughts and plans—you choke the budding plants of your mentality. But, if you let pour forth a full, abiding, confident Faith in yourself—your abilities, your qualities, your latent powers, your desires, your plans— your Success, in short—you will find that the whole mental garden responds to the stimulating influence; and ideas, thoughts, plans and other mental flowers will spring up rapidly. There is nothing so stimulating as a strong, positive "I Can and I Will" attitude toward oneself.

And you remember what has been said about the Law of Attraction—you remember how "like attracts like," and how one's Mental Attitude tends to draw toward him the things in harmony with his thoughts.

Well, this being so, can you not see that a Mental Attitude of Faith or Confidence in Oneself is calculated to attract to you that which fits in with such Faith—that will tend to materialize your ideal?

"Confidence is the basis of all trade"; so says one of our recent business philosophers, and this statement is true; for if we did not have Confidence or Faith in our Fellowman, all trade, all business, all commerce would come to a standstill. The wholesale merchant ships yearly hundreds of thousands of dollars' worth of goods to dealers in his territory. He has Faith that in thirty, sixty or ninety days those dealers will pay their bills and he will reap his profits. You go to the retail dealer and buy a suit, or dress, or hat, or groceries, having the same charged to your account. Your dealer has Confidence or Faith enough in you to let you have these goods, expecting that you will pay your bill when it falls due. This same rule holds good in almost every transaction in life. You must have confidence in a man before you care to deal with him.

Some people seem to be of a naturally suspicious frame of mind, always of the opinion that somebody else is trying to "do" them. Others are gullible and swallow everything—bait, hook and line. Neither is the wisest frame of mind. It is much better to maintain the thought of good-will, fellowship, and confidence towards one's fellowman, weighing all things impartially from an unprejudiced standpoint, and then render your decision after due thought from the facts in the case. But, by all means, have faith in your Fellowman.

But, this Faith in Oneself, and Faith in your Fellowman, important though they be, are not the only kinds of Faith that one needs in order to attain Financial Success. There is that which may be called Faith in the *Law*. This may seem a little strange to you but when you consider it for a moment, you will see just how it operates.

You will note that nearly all successful men have a deep-rooted belief in Something Outside that helps them along. They do not know just what this

Something is—some call it "Luck"; some call it their "Destiny"; some call it their "Star"; and why not? But under all of these names there is an instructive belief in, and faith in a Something Friendly that helps them along, and carries them over the hard places, and rounds the sharp corners of business life. Watch any successful man, and you will see that even when he is not able to reason out the means whereby he is going to get over, or around, or under a set of difficulties, still he exhibits a hopeful faith and belief that he is "going to get through it somehow." And he does, if he holds on to his Faith. Something is there at work tending to "pull him through," Ask any successful business man if this is not so. And this Something that successful men intuitively trust in is nothing but the great *Law* that underlies all of the affairs of Life. The nearer that one can feel in contact with this *Law*, more power does he receive from it. And thus Faith is the underlying channel by which the Power of the *Law* is transmitted to you.

Why should you Fear? You seat yourself in a train or street-car, and read your paper, having Faith that the engineer or motorman will take you to your destination. You manifest this Faith in every-day business life. Without Faith in the Whole Thing, business would be impossible. You manifest Faith at every turn of the road. And this being so, why should you not manifest Faith in the underlying *Law* which is manifesting in things? Do you suppose for an instant that this whole Cosmic Machinery is run by Chance? There is no such thing as Chance! Everything is run under some great *Law*! And the Law of Financial Success is just as much a part of that great system of *Law* as is the Law of Gravitation. You study the Laws of physical life, and find them invariable, and therefore worthy of bestowing Faith upon. Why should you not recognize the great Mental Laws operative in business life, and acquaint yourself with their workings? Why should you not have Faith in them? There is no better plan of bringing yourself into harmony with the Law of Financial Success, than to recognize and have Faith in it. Consider the careers of successful business men of your acquaintance, and see if this is not so. By doing so you will receive a new light on a heretofore dark subject.

# Latent Powers

In beginning this chapter, I am reminded of the words of Lovell: "There are infinite powers lying dormant in man, here, now—powers which, could he but catch a glimpse of, would endow his life on this planet with greater splendor, and impart to it a redoubled interest"

The man who regards himself as a creature built on a certain mental plan, and incapable of any material change beyond an improvement of the faculties already being expressed, sees but a small portion of the truth regarding himself and his possibilities. Very few men express or manifest more than a small part of their latent power. They live long lives and go down to their graves without suspecting that within their mental kingdom there had reposed dormant faculties, and latent powers which, if expressed, would have enabled them to have lived far wider, broader, fuller lives.

Nearly every man who has attained success along any of the varied lines of human endeavor will tell you that at some period of his life he was called upon to assume certain responsibilities—undertake some unaccustomed task—play some unfamiliar part on life's stage—and then much to his surprise found that he had within him the power, capability, and qualifications for a successful accomplishment of the strange task. The crucial point was when he was brought face to face with the new undertaking. If, as is the case with the majority of man, be lacked nerve enough to say "I Can and I Will," the story was ended. But if he had that Something within him which enabled him to assert his determination to face the thing manfully and at least to go down with his flags flying rather than to run away, he would find much to his surprise that there was within him a power which responded to the needs of the hour and which enabled him to master the undertaking.

These experiences are not exceptional or unusual— they are part of the common experience of nearly all successful men. And successful men get to realize that they have within them, hidden in some of the many recesses of the mind, latent powers, unsuspected talents, and dormant faculties which are awaiting calmly the hour of their call to action. The human mind is far from being the simple everyday thing that man regards it. There are hidden chambers, and unexplored regions. Science is just beginning to learn some of these heretofore unsuspected truths about the mind, and the result is dazzling the observer whose eyes are suddenly seeing the brilliant truths. There seem to be within every man possibilities of which he has never even dreamed. There seem to be capabilities, the extent of which has never entered into even his wildest imagination. Some sudden call, some new responsibility, some new turn of fortune's tide, and the man is called upon to demand of his mentality all that it is holding in store for him—and he is seldom disappointed, providing he has the nerve and courage to make the demand. Aye, but there's the rub—few have that courage and nerve. Have YOU?

I know personally a man whose life up to the age of thirty-eight had been spent in active business and professional life. The thought of writing for the public had never occurred to him. All of a sudden, by one of those strange upheavals that come into the lives of men, all was carried away from him. His health was shattered, his accumulations were swept away, he was apparently lifted up and placed in a new, strange and seemingly unpromising environment. He had his family to support—he had practically nothing left with which to do it. His health was broken, and it was impossible for him to re-engage in his accustomed occupation. While building up his health, he helped a new friend to get the mechanical part of a monthly magazine in shape. At the last moment his friend discovered that they were short several pages of matter, and the printers were impatiently asking for their full supply. The friend was too busily occupied to write the additional matter, and so in desperation, he turned to my friend and said, "Did you ever write anything for publication?" "No," was the answer." Well, somebody has got to write something, and mighty quick, too. Have you nerve enough to try it?" "Yes," was the reply. "I'm like the boy digging for woodchuck, who was asked whether he expected to catch it, and who replied, "You bet I do—we've got the preacher for dinner, and no meat in the house—I've just got to catch that woodchuck." And so like the boy, I've just got to, and I Can and I Will" And he did.

He sat down to write to fill that space, although he had never written a line for publication before. He made a mighty effort of his Will, urged on by an imperative Desire, and almost in a daze he found his hand at work writing, easily and rapidly. Before long the article was turned out—and it was good. This success led to others, and that man has been writing books, editing magazines, and doing other work of that kind for the past seven years, and he has been successful all along the line. Within six months after the incident noted above, he had completed a book that has since ran through over twenty editions. And since then he has written and had published over a dozen other books on various subjects, none of which has failed to reach his public and all of which have ran through a number of editions. Inside of two years after the above incident, he was editing a magazine, built up by his writings, and which attained a circulation of over one hundred thousand per month.

And yet this man had never written a line up to that time. An apparent chance opportunity caused him to face the question, "Can You?" And instead of saying, "Oh, no, I've never done that kind of work—it is impossible," he answered like the boy after the woodchuck: "I've just got to—I Can and I Will" He met the crucial test—had nerve enough to tackle the seemingly impossible proposition, and then found within himself unsuspected power, strength and ability—and won out.

Is this merely a lesson in facing difficulties, and cultivating nerve and self-confidence? Not entirely—it teaches these things and also teaches the still greater truth that every man has within himself wonderful powers, lying dormant and unsuspected, which are merely awaiting the word of the master Will, impelled by a burning, eager, ardent desire, to spring at once into being, full armed and equipped for the fray. And these powers and capabilities come under the *Law*—they are a part of that great Something behind, underneath, and within us all. The recognition of the existence of such powers is the first step toward their development and unfoldment.

You think that you have not ability for Financial Success, simply because you do not realize the existence of these latent powers within you. If you were brought suddenly face to face with the necessity of awakening these powers into action, and could muster up enough courage to say "I Can and I Will," you would find the ready response from within, and the steady flow of knowledge, wisdom, power and ability with which to accomplish the task set before you for completion.

And so my parting words for this chapter are: Do not hesitate to accept any new responsibility, whether the same is forced upon you, or whether you reach out for it yourself. Say to yourself over and over again, "I can and I will accomplish this task. It never would have been put before me unless I were able." And you will be surprised and delighted at the new and wonderful powers that will spring forth from your subconscious self to aid you in your undertaking.

These are not mere idle words, designed to make pleasant reading. They are the words of truths that have become apparent to every successful man or woman. Talk with the successful people of the world, and they will tell you that they have had this experience over and over again—new opportunities and new necessities brought to them new faculties, and new powers, heretofore undreamed of. The demand always brings the supply, if we will but open ourselves to the inflow from the great Source of Supply—the Universal Power House.

# Ambition

"*Ambition*"—what a glorious word! How the very sound of it stirs one's energies, and makes one feel the inspiration to be up and at work doing things, succeeding, creating, accomplishing!

And what does Ambition really, mean, pray? It means more than a mere eagerness for things. It means the deep-seated desire to materialize certain ideals which exist in the mind as mental pictures. Before one can accomplish things he must be possessed of Ambition. And before he can feel Ambition he must have the preceding hunger which causes him to manifest Ambition with which to satisfy it. And so it follows, anything that will stimulate that mental hunger, will arouse Ambition, and thus create that eagerness for action and attainment. And how may that mental hunger be produced?

There is a psychological law underlying this mental hunger that manifests as Ambition. And that law is:—that in order for that mental hunger to be manifested it must have ideals presented to the mind's eye. Just as the gastric juices of the stomach may be stimulated and caused to flow by the sight, smell, or thought of food, so is this mental hunger produced by the sight, thought or idea of the things needed for its satisfaction. If you are contented with your present life, and want nothing better, it is chiefly because you know nothing better—have seen nothing better—have heard of nothing better, or else you are mentally and physically lazy. The ignorant savage seeking to till his land by means of a sharpened stick, cannot desire a steel plow or other agricultural implement if he does not know of them. He simply keeps right at work in his old way—the way of his forefathers—and feels no desire for a better implement. But by-and-by some man comes along with a steel plow, and our savage opens his eyes in wide surprise at the wonderful thing. If he be a savage of discernment be begins to get up an interest in the new thing. He watches it at work, and sees how much better it accomplishes the task than does his crude pointed stick. If he be a progressive savage, he begins to wish he had one of the strange new implements, and if he wants it hard enough he begins to experience a new, strange feeling of mental hunger for the thing, which if sufficiently strong, causes his Ambition to bud.

And this is the critical point. Up to this time he has felt the strong Desire preceding Ambition. But now with the dawn of Ambition comes the arousing of the Will. And this is what Ambition is, A Strong Will Aroused by a Strong Desire.

Without these two elements there can be no Ambition. Desire without Will is not Ambition. One may want a thing very hard, but if he does not arouse his Will strongly enough to actively co-operate with the Desire, his Ambition will "die a-borning." And though one's Will be as strong as steel, yet if there be not strong Desire animating and inspiring it, it will not manifest as Ambition.

To manifest Ambition fully, one must first eagerly desire the thing—not a mere "wanting" or "wishing" for it, but a fierce, eager, consuming hunger which demands satisfaction. And then one must have a Will aroused sufficiently strong to go out and get that which Desire is demanding. These two elements constitute the activity of Ambition.

Look around you at the successful men of the world in any line of human effort and endeavor, and you will see that they all have Ambition strongly developed. They have the fierce craving of Desire for things, and the firm Will which will brook no interference with the satisfaction of the Desire. Study the lives of Caesar, Napoleon, and their modern counterparts, the Twentieth Century Captains of Industry, and you will see the glare of this fierce Ambition burning brightly and hotly within them.

The trouble with the majority of the people if that they have been taught that one should take what was given him and be content. But this is not Nature's way. Nature implants in each living being a strong desire for that which is necessary for its wellbeing and nourishment, and a strong will to gratify that natural desire. On all sides in Nature, you may see this law in effect. The plant and the animal obey it, and are not afraid. But Man, as he ascended the scale of evolution, while seeing the necessity and advantage of curbing and restraining certain tendencies and desires, which if freely gratified would work harm on himself and upon society, has swung to the other extreme. In cutting off the dead branches of Desire, he has lopped off some live ones at the same time—that is, the majority of men have—the few who haven't reach out and gather to themselves the good things of life, throwing the "cores" and leavings to the rest.

There is no earthly reason why a man should not earnestly desire the good things of life—no reason why he should not stimulate that fierce hunger for attainment by painting mental pictures of what he needs—by looking upon the good things in the world in the possession of others, so that he can see what he wants. "But does this not arouse covetousness?" you may ask. Not at all—you are not coveting the things the others have, but are merely desiring other things like them. You are willing that these other people should retain their things, but are demanding similar good things for yourself. This is not covetousness, but laudable Ambition.

And laudable Ambition is all right There is enough of the good things of live in this world for all of us, if we demand them, and reach out for them. Demand causes supply, in and under the *Law*, so be not afraid. Arouse your Ambition—it is a good thing and not something of which to be ashamed. Urge it on—feed it—stimulate its growth. It is not a foul weed, but a strong, vigorous, healthy plant in the garden of life, bearing more fruit than any other growing thing there.

Do not let the argument that men have used Ambition to accomplish evil ends disconcert you. Every natural law is capable of being used for good or evil. Because any law has been used for evil, it is no reason why those who desire to do good should avoid it, and refrain from using it for right purposes. To do so would be like the Angels of Light running away and leaving the powers of darkness in possession of all the good things of the world. The best way is to grasp the weapon and turn it against the enemy.

The *Law* is there awaiting man's use. If you prefer to leave it for the evil disposed persons, very well, that is your own loss. But the wise, the sane, the strong men of the day are now reaching out for the use of the *Law* and are accomplishing great things by reason of it. When the Many use the *Law*, the Few will cease to be the sole possessors of the good things of life, which alas! so many of them have misused. When the secret is generally known, the evil will be eradicated and good will supersede it.

Therefore, be not afraid to stand boldly out, crying: "I want this, and I am going to have it! It is my rightful heritage, and I demand it of the *Law*!" Be ambitious to attain financial Success because that is the goal for which you are striving.

# Desire

In some of the previous chapters I have spoken of the operation of Desire and Will in the manifestation and expression of personal power under the *Law*. Now, while there have been many writers who have discoursed ably regarding the mighty power of the Will, there have been but few who have given to the subject of Desire the attention that it deserves, and the consideration it merits. Many persons seem afraid to speak of Desire, for they have gotten the term and idea mixed up with desires of an unworthy and detrimental nature. They have overlooked the fact that Desire must underlie all human action—must be the causing power back of and underneath Will itself.

We might compare Desire with the fire that burns brightly beneath the receptacle containing water, which latter represents the mind. Unless the fire of Desire burns brightly and imparts its heat to the water, or mind, there will be nothing but water. But let the fire manifest its ardent energy and heat, and lo! the water is converted into steam which turns mighty wheels, and drives powerful machinery, and in fact "makes things go." We are apt to forget the causes that have operated in order that the steam be produced, in our wonder, amazement and admiration of the power and effect of the manifested steam. But, in order to get the right idea of the matter fixed in our mind we must take into consideration the water of the mind, and the fire of Desire.

The mind is well represented by water, for it is unstable, changeable, in motion, having eddies, storms, ripples and calm. And Desire is well represented by fire, for it is ardent, hot, strong and burning, and when manifested properly invariably acts upon the water-mind and produce the will-steam which may be turned to the accomplishment of any task, and the moving of the material necessary for our plans. By all means keep the fire of Desire brightly burning under your mental boilers, and you will be sure to manifest the proper amount and degree of the steam of Will which may then be applied to the accomplishing of your life tasks.

If you will keep the figure of speech before your mind—this idea of the fire of desire, the water of the mind, and the steam of will—you will find it easier to put into operation these great mental forces, and to be known as the man or woman of the "Strong Will." But if you allow the fire of Desire to burn low, or to become clogged with the ashes of dead and gone things, long since exhausted and useless, you will find that there will be little or no steam of will produced, and you will be in the position of the majority of people who are like tea kettles simmering over a faint fire, and accomplishing nothing.

Unless you want a thing "the worst way," and manifest that Desire in the shape of a strong impelling force, you will have no will with which to accomplish anything. You must not only "want" to do a thing, or to possess a thing, but you must "want to hard."

You must want it as the Hungry man wants bread, as the smothering man wants air. And if you will but arouse in your self this fierce, ardent, insatiate Desire, you will set in operation one of Nature's most potent mental forces.

What is that great impelling force that you have felt within yourself whenever you have made a mighty effort to accomplish something? Is it not that surging, restless, impelling force of your being that you know as Desire? Did you do the thing simply because you thought it best, or because you felt within yourself a strong feeling that you *Wanted* to do the thing, or to possess the thing, in the strongest possible way? Did you not feel this strong force of Desire rising within you and impelling you to deed, and action?

Desire is the great moving power of the Mind—that which excites into action the will and powers of the individual. It is at the bottom of all action, feeling, emotion or expression. Before we reach out to do a thing, or to possess a thing, we must first "want to," and in the degree that that "want-to" is felt, so will be our response thereto. Before we love, hate, like or dislike, there must be a Desire of some kind. Before we can arouse ambition there must be a strong Desire. Before we can manifest energy, there must a strong impelling Desire.

Did you ever stop to think that the difference between the strong of the race, and the weak, is largely a matter of Desire? The degree of Desire manifests in the different degrees of strength and weakness. The strong men of the race are filled with strong desires to do this thing, or to possess that. They are filled with that strong creative Desire that makes them want to build up, create, modify, change, and shift around. It is not alone the fruits of their labor that urge them on, but that insistent urge of the creative Desire that drives them on.

Do not be afraid to allow your Desire for Financial Success to burn brightly. Keep the ashes of part failures, disappointments and discouragements well cleared away so that you may have a good draught. Keep the fire of Desire burning brightly, ardently and constantly. Do not be sidetracked by outside things, for remember, concentrated Desire is that which produces the greatest steam-producing power. Keep your mind fixed on that which you want, and keep on demanding that which belongs to you, for it is your own. The Universal Supply is adequate for all needs of everyone, but it responds only to the insistent demand and the earnest Desire. Learn to Desire things in earnest. and rest not content with a mere wanting and wishing.

Desire creates Mental Attitude—develops Faith—nourishes Ambition—unfolds Latent Powers—and tends directly and surely toward Success. Let the strong, dominant desire for Financial Independence possess you from the tips of your toes to the roots of your hair,—feel it forging through every part of your body—and then don't stop until you reach your goal.

# Will Power

"O well for him whose Will is strong!," writes Tennyson, and the poets of all nations and times have sung the same song. Tennyson well voices this human regard and admiration for the power of the Will He tells us again; "O living Will, thou shalt endure, when all that seems shall suffer shock."

The Will of man if a strange, subtle, intangible, and yet very real thing that is closely connected with the inmost essence of his "I." When the "I" acts, it acts through the Will. The Will is the immediate expression of the Ego, or "I" in Man, which rests at the very seat of his being. This Ego, or "I" within each of us—that inmost self of each one of us—expresses itself in two ways. It first asserts "I Am" by which it expresses its existence and reality; then it asserts "I Will," by which it expresses its desire to act, and its determination to do so. The "I Will" comes right from the center of your being, and is the strongest expression of the Great Life Force within you. And in the degree that you cultivate and express it, is the degree of positivity that you manifest. The person of weak Will is a negative, cringing weakling, while he of strong Will is the positive, courageous, masterful individual in whom Nature delights and whom she rewards.

The human Will is an actual living force. It is just as much an active force of Nature as is Electricity, Magnetism, or any other form of natural force. Will is as real an Energy as is gravitation. From atom to man, desire and Will are in evidence—first comes the desire to do a thing, and then comes the Will that does it. It is an invariable law pervading all natural forms, shapes, degrees of things—animate and inanimate.

Nothing is impossible to the man who can Will—providing he can Will sufficiently strong. And as Will depends so very much upon one's belief in his ability, it may be said that all action depends upon belief. One does not Will unless he believes that he has a Will. And many a man of inherent strong Will does not express it or exert it, simply because he does not realize that he possesses it. It is only when the necessity arises from some new unexpected demand for the exercise of the Will, that many men realize that they really possess such a Will. To many, alas, such a necessity never comes.

In speaking about the Will, I do not mean stubbornness. You will find plenty of people who are as stubborn as mules and their friends and neighbors will say that "they are strong-willed," meaning by this that when they decide a thing "is so, it's so, and you can't make me believe it isn't." This is the mulish attitude of mind coming from prejudice or ignorance and has nothing to do with the Will. The man with the strong Will knows when to recede from his petition as well as when to go forward; he never stands still. When the occasion warrants it, he steps back, but only for the purpose of getting a better start, for he always has a definite goal in view. When the command from within calls him to go forward, he drives right ahead like the mighty ocean steamer, majestic in his power and stopping for nothing. This frame of mind is best illustrated by the following quotation written of Howard the philanthropist:

"The energy of his determination was so great, that if instead of being habitual, it had been shown only for a short time on particular occasions, it would have appeared a vehement impetuosity; but, by being unintermitted, it had an equability of manner which scarcely appeared to exceed the tone of a calm constancy, it was so totally the reverse of anything like turbulence or agitation. It was the calmness of an intensity, kept uniform by the nature of the human mind forbidding it to be more, and by the character of the individual forbidding it to be less."

The subject of the development of the Will is too large for a single chapter of any book. It is the study of a lifetime. Several fine books have been written covering the subject fairly well, but the best so far, are two recent books by Haddock, "Power of Will" and "Power for Success" which contain the essence of about everything ever written on the subject that is of value to one who desires development along these lines. Buy and study these books by all means.

The writer believes that the basis of all personal power resides in the Will and that if one intends to accomplish anything in this world he must acquire a powerful Will. The best way to do this is to first recognize your lack, and then by constant affirmations of "I can and I will accomplish this thing," and by the repetition of selections on the Will, taken from the best literature, build up within yourself, little by little, an invincible power and energy that will overcome every temptation to sidetrack you from your life purpose. At the end of this chapter I have appended some excellent selections and others you will find scattered throughout the book. These selections can be memorized and then repeated in times of trial and discouragement and they will prove invigorating tonic for the depressed mind.

The proper attitude of the student of the Law of Financial Success is that mental attitude which may best be expressed as the *"I Can and I Will"* state of mind. In this mental attitude there are combined the two primary elements of the accomplishment of things. First there comes that belief in one's ability, power, and force which begets confidence, and which causes to make a clear mental channel over which the Will flows. Then, second, comes the assertion of the Will itself—the *"I WILL"* part of it. When a man says *"I Will"* with all the force and energy and determination of his character being poured into it, then does his Will become a very Dynamic Force which sweeps away obstacles before it in its mighty onrush.

Not only does this expression of the Will stir into activity the latent powers and dormant energies of the man's mind, bringing to the accomplishment of the task all his reserve force, power and strength, but it does much more. It impresses those around him with a mighty psychical power which compels attention to his words and demands recognition for himself. In all conflicts between men, the strongest Will wins the day. The struggle may be short, or it may be long, but the end is the same always—the man of the strongest Will wins.

And not only does the awakened Will do this, but it also acts in the direction of affecting those at a distance from the person. It sets in motion certain natural laws which tend to compel things toward the center occupied by a mighty Will. Look around you, and you will see that the men of giant Wills set up a strong center of influence, which extends on all sides in all directions, affecting this one and that one, and drawing and compelling others to fall in with the movements instigated by that Will. There are men who set up great whirlpools or whirlwinds of Will, which are felt by persons far and near. And, in fact all persons who exert Will at all, do this to a greater or lesser extent, depending upon the degree of Will expressed.

Read, study, and absorb the following selections:

"The education of the Will is the object of our existence."

They can who think they can. Character is a perfectly educated Will"

"Nothing can resist the Will of a man who knows what is true and wills what is good."

"To will evil is to will death. A perverse Will is the beginning of suicide."

In all difficulties advance and Will, for within you is a Power, a living Force which, the more you trust and learn to use, will annihilate the opposition of matter."

"The star of the unconquered Will,
He rises in my breast,
Serene and resolute and still,
And calm and self-possessed."

"So nigh is grandeur to our dust, So near is God to man, When Duty whispers low, "Thou must!" The youth replies, 'I can.' "

"I will to will with energy and decision! I will to persist in willing! I will to will intelligently and for a goal! I will to exercise the will in accordance with the dictates of reason and of morals."

"The human will, that force unseen, The offspring of a deathless soul, Can hew a way to any goal Though walls of granite intervene.

"You will be what you will to be, Let failure find its false content In that poor word environment, But spirit scorns it and its free.

"It masters time, it conquers space,
It cows that boastful trickster, chance, And bids the tyrant circumstance Uncrown and fill a servant's place."

"There is no chance, no destiny, no fate. Can circumvent, or hinder, or control
The firm resolve of a determined soul. Gifts count for nothing, will alone in great; All things give way before it soon or late.
What obstacle can stay the mighty force Of the sea-seeking river in its course, Or cause the ascending orb of day to wait?
Each well-born soul must win what it deserves, Let the fools prate of lack. The fortunate he whose earnest purpose never swerves,
Whose slightest action, or inaction
Serves the one great aim. Why, even Death itself Stands still and waits an hour sometimes For such a will."

# Auto-Suggestion

You will have noticed that in the preceding chapters I have begun a serious campaign in the direction of having you "make yourself over" mentally, in order to bring you under the operation of the Law of Financial Success. You will remember that first I tried to get you to regard Money in a new light—as a natural supply akin to the nourishment of the plant, and coming under the same general law of Natural Supply and Demand.

Second—I urged upon you to build up the proper Mental Attitude, showing you how by so doing you would cultivate in yourself the faculties, qualities and powers conducive to success; the qualities likely to attract and influence people with whom you come in contact; and the mental state which would set into operation the beneficent phases of the Law of Attraction.

Third—I proceeded to get Fear and Worry out of your mental system.

Fourth—I went on to cultivate the quality of Faith in you.

Fifth—came the consideration of the Latent Powers and the roles for their unfoldment.

Sixth—came the explanation of the nature of Ambition, and the urge to cultivate and develop it.

Seventh—came the explanation of the wonderful effect and office of Desire, and the advice to cultivate Desire as a means of cultivating Will.

Eighth—I gave you instruction for the development of a powerful Will, the acquirement of which means so much to you.

Now, if you will stop a moment, you will see that the practical application of the instruction given and the precepts laid down for your guidance require a certain "making over" of yourself, on your part.

This being so the question arises: "How may I best accomplish the 'making-over' process?" And to answer this question, I shall now devote several chapters, for in the answering lies much of the essence of this instruction that I am desirous of imparting to you. And so this is the reason that we now take up the subject of "Auto-Suggestion," a subject of the greatest importance to you, and which has engaged the minds of scientific men for the past few years. Let as hasten to a consideration of the subject.

In the first place the term "Suggestion," as used by psychologists means "an impression made upon the mind of another." And an "auto-suggestion" is an impression made upon one's own mind in a manner similar to that used in impressing the mind of another. You will see this a little clearer in a moment. The whole essence of Suggestion lies in the idea of "impression." Think of the mind as a wax substance, and the Suggestion as a die making an impression on the wax, and there you have it.

If you can manage to get in a strong Suggestion on the mind of a person, you really impress your notion or idea upon his mental wax, so to speak. Suggestion it not of matter of argumentative effort, but a process of saying a thing so positively, earnestly and convincingly that the other person takes up the idea without argument. We may be impressed by a man's earnestness, his manner, his attitude, his dress, and in many other ways, but the principle is the same—if we are impressed by something about him, we have taken the Suggestion. Do you see what I mean?

Well, one may turn this Suggestive die upon the wax of his own mind and by repeated impressions may fix certain ideas, qualities, and characteristics upon it so that he will have really made himself over to that extent. It is a case of "sez I to myself, sez I"— often repeated until "I" believes what "I sez." You know how a man may get to actually believe some old lie that he has been telling for some time. A man may act out a certain assumed character, until he actually becomes like the character. There are plenty of old chaps strutting around today with these assumed characters, which not only fool the people with whom they come in contact, but also actually fool the men themselves. Now if this be true about things of this kind, how important does the principle become when applied to the creation of new characteristics and qualities in oneself that are conducive to success. You all know just about the ones you need, and now here it the way to go about getting them.

To many people Auto-Suggestion means simply the repeating of certain words to themselves, like "I am Energetic—I am Ambitions," etc. etc. Now this plan is all very well, for a constant impression of this kind will undoubtedly tend to develop the suggested qualities in one. But there is a far more scientific plan known to psychologists, and that is the one I am going to urge upon your consideration. It is that not only should one "say" things to himself, but that he should also create Mental Images of the desired thing, and should also act out the part he wishes to play, in a sort of extended preliminary rehearsal.

All this may seem odd to you unless you have studied the psychological principles underlying it, which I have not time to go into here. The thing to remember is that constant thinking of a desired quality of mind, accompanied with the indulgence in the Mental Picture of yourself as actually possessed of the quality itself, and also accompanied by an "acting out" of the part you would like to play, will in due time so impress and mold your mind that you will actually possess the quality itself. Here is a great psychological law I have expressed. Read it again, study it, and make it your own.

For instance let us suppose that you lack Ambition. Well, the first thing is to rouse the Desire to become Ambitious. Then start in the plan of "sez I to myself, sez I," and make constant affirmation of the fact that: "I am Ambitious—very Ambitious—my Ambition grows every day," and so on. Then picture yourself in your imagination as being Ambitious—see yourself as moving around in the world possessed of an insatiable Ambition which is leading you to strenuous action and wonderful accomplishments. Then begin to act out the part of the Ambitious man—study some Ambitious man until you catch his feelings and then begin to look Ambitious; talk in the tones of a man possessing Ambition; walk like an Ambitious man—in short act out the part to the smallest details. Now remember I do not mean to copy the mannerisms of the man you have taken for your model—this is not the thing at all. Simply study him until you can get his feelings—until you can recognize the Ambitious emotion and Mental Attitude animating him, and then go to work to feel the same inward feeling yourself, and to act out the feeling. If you can once get the feeling, then all you've got to do is to act it out right.

You will find that this plan of mental discipline and exercise may be used for the acquirement of any and every one of the positive qualities you may desire to acquire and possess. This is no mere theory, but is a scientific fact known to and taught by some of the leading authorities on the subject in the world. It has been the basis of the making over of thousands of people, some of whom have paid enormous fees to teachers for just this plain advice, elaborated and padded out into long series of personal lectures and lessons. I offer you something here that is well "worth while." Now it is for you to take it and use it.

# Harmony

All through Nature, and Nature's manifestations, there exists rhythm and Harmony. Everything in the Universe is in unceasing action. There is a universal vibratory movement apparent everywhere. From the atoms, and the particles composing the atoms, up through all the material combinations and groupings there is constant, incessant vibration and motion. And from this constant motion, and running through its entire manifestation, there is apparent a constant and invariable law of rhythm. Just as there is a rhythm apparent in all that we call music, so is there a rhythm in the music of Nature. And from that rhythm proceeds that which we call Harmony.

The planets as they swing in regular orbits around the sun—yes, the suns as they swing around still greater suns—and so on until the mind fails to grasp the wonder of it all—all manifest rhythm. The sea in its manifestation of the rise and fall of the tides, exhibits rhythm. The heart of man breathes in rhythmic measure. In the great waves of light traveling to us from the sun and stars, millions upon millions of miles away, there exists a rhythmic measure registered upon the delicate instruments of science.

You have heard of the wonderful force latent in the rhythmic measure of music. You have read of instances in which mighty bridges have been shattered by the note of the violin constantly sounded in an uninterrupted rhythm. It seems almost incredible, but it is true that the soft note of a tiny violin, constantly sounded in regular rhythm can become powerful enough to make the bridge first tremble, and then shudder, and then sway to and fro until it finally collapses. Science teaches us that even the mighty steel skyscrapers of our great cities could be brought to the ground in a mass of twisted steel rods, if one were but to ascertain the keynote of the entire building, and then manage to start into motion the vibrations of a strong musical instrument, constantly sounding that one keynote, over and over again, for hour after hour, until the great giant structure would "catch the motion" and begin to tremble.

"To catch the motion," that is it. If we could but "catch the motion" of Nature's great rhythmic harmony we could accomplish anything. And this is not such a wild dream as might be supposed at first glance. There is a great rhythmic harmony inherent in the mind of man. Just as the bridge has its keynote, so has the mind of each man, and the great mind of the race of men. And if we will but withdraw ourselves from the incidents and distractions of the outer life and retire for a moment or two within the inner regions of ourselves, we may catch the faint echo of that great Universal Harmony of the mind, sounding clear and well defined. If we can do this, we have but to take up the mental keynote and sound it until we make our influence felt.

Men of the busy world—the "practical" men of our day—are beginning to realize this fact, and we hear strange stories of such men closing their private office doors for a few moments during the day, and communing with themselves, withdrawing their attention from the distracting thoughts and scenes of the outside world. This is no mere transcendental idea, but a fact that many shrewd business men of the day are turning to good account.

Remember, that "in quietness there is strength," Every person who is ambitions and has a definite object in life should take a few minutes off each day, and sit alone, giving himself a chance to think, meditate, and allow the great rhythmic harmony of Nature to flow through his cleared mind, and thus gain renewed strength and energy. It is in these quiet moments, when the outer mind is relaxed and resting, that the inner mind flashes to us that which is best for as to do. We should cultivate this habit in moments of meditation, when we may escape from the people and crowd, and thus be able to listen to the voice that sounds from within. By doing this we place ourselves in harmony with the great Universal Power from which all original ideas spring into our mental organism ready for use a few moments later when we re-emerge into the world of action and of men.

Here are a few directions for entering into harmony with the Universal Rhythm of Nature: First, your mental attitude must be right You must have gained control of your thoughts and words, to that your mind is open and receptive to the great good of the world. There must be no hate there, no discouragement, no pessimism, no negative, cringing, worm-of-the-dust or poverty thought—your frame of mind must be that of good-will, encouragement, optimum, with positive thoughts expectant of wealth, prosperity, and all the good things that man, heir of the universe, is entitled to by right of his sonship. This latter mental attitude will surround you with a personal thought atmosphere which repels from you the negative or evil things and attracts to you the positive or good things of life.

When you are satisfied that your personal atmosphere is right, then each day, preferably between twelve and one o'clock, or if that time it not convenient, early in the morning just after your bath, close the doors of your room, shutting out everybody and everything for a few moments. Take precautions that you shall not be disturbed, and then put away from your mind the fear of interruption and disturbance. Take a position of restful and peaceful calm. Relax every muscle, and take the tension off of every nerve. Take a few deep restful breaths, which will seem like great sighs, and will tend to relax your body and mind. Then detach your thoughts from the outer world, and things, and turn the mind inward upon yourself. Shut out all the material cares, worries and problems of the day and sink into a mental state of peaceful calm. Think "I open myself to the inflow of the Universal Rhythmic Harmony" and you will soon begin to feel a sense of relationship with that Harmony coming into you, filling your mind and body with a feeling of rest and peace, and latent power. Then shortly after will come to you a sense of new strength and energy, and a desire to once more emerge upon the scene of your duties. This is the time for you to close the meditation. Do not seek to prolong it, but go forth with your new energy, filled with the vibrations of the Universal, and you will see how refreshed and vigorous you are, and how your mind leaps eagerly and enthusiastically to the tasks before it.

Oh yes!, all this does belong to the subject of Financial Success as you will find out if you will practice a little and discover the secret of the silence as given above. If you doubt it and smile with a quizzical, know-it-all smile then you are the one who needs it most. Just remember that this is not written by some wild theorist soaring in the clouds of hazy metaphysics, but by a business man—part of it during business hours amidst the cares, duties, and exactions of a strenuous business life—who has applied these principles and knows whereof he speaks.

I shall now tell you a secret known only to a few. From this time on it is yours. See that you use it. Here it is: A few moments spent with your inner self and the Great Universal Power each day, as described above, if practiced assiduously, will establish within you the Creative Mind—that wonderful thing which marks the difference between the Italian ditch digger, who plods along from day to day with never a new idea for his own or humanity's betterment, and the man "at the top" who "does things"; the constructive man who builds railroads, steamships, large mercantile establishments, and who furnishes funds to carry the great work of the world along. Both of these men are needed, but it feels better to be near the top. The more you practice, the more you will open up that great subconscious reservoir of yours which is overflowing with original ideas. In time you will gain the power to get in touch with your inner self and tap that reservoir wherever you may be—in the street car— out for a walk—while you are shaving—and there will flash through to your conscious mind, in vivid outlines, ideas that when worked out will mean for you Money and Financial Independence.

# Creation

The title of this chapter may appear strange to some of those who find it in a book entitled "The Law of Financial Success," and such people may wonder what in the world "Creation" has to do with the subject of Financial Success. I ask such persons to wait patiently until the chapter is finished, and I promise to do my best to convince these doubters that Creation has very much to do with the attainment of Financial Success, and that, in fact, there can be little or no Financial Success without the operation of the creative energy of the mind.

Did you ever stop to think that in the case of some of the mighty bridges spanning the rivers surrounding New York City, each span, each strand of steel, each support, each bit of construction—and the whole bridge in its entirety—existed and was created in the mind of the designer before it was manifested or materialized?

Did you ever think that the great buildings which rear their imposing forms and shapes along our business streets were created in the minds of their architects, and actually existed in their minds before the buildings could be erected?

Did you ever think that the delicate mechanism of the watch you are carrying in your pocket existed in the mind of its designer long before the material watch was evolved from the parts? The watch would not be, and could not be, unless the designer had seen it all in his mind's eye, down to the smallest detail, before he materialized it.

The above statements are more or less common-place, but the majority of people overlook these important facts in the contemplation of material things. They ignore the fact that anything and everything that has ever been created in material form must of necessity have been created in mental form previously. There is no exception to this rule. Everything that is materialized must have existed previously in the mind of the person creating it. The house, the bridge, the watch, the suit of clothes, the hat, the pen-knife, the shoes, the buttons on the clothes—everything that you can see, or think of, that has been made, has first been created mentally, in its every part and as a whole.

When we materialize a thing by creating or building it, we simply build the material around the mental picture of the thing that we have first created. The primal building is in the mind. And this is true of Financial Success just as it is true of everything else. Some build little by little, seeing only just a little in advance of their building, and thus do their mental creation by piece-meal. Others see the whole thing in general outline and then fill in the details as they go along. The principle is the same in both cases.

It is told of Thomas Lawson, of Boston—he of Frenzied Finance" fame—that when he was a youth he painted a mental picture of a large estate on which there was the finest breed of horses, and the choicest cattle in the world; a beautiful home furnished and filled with objects of artistic value; and everything else necessary for the completion of his conception of an ideal home. He has said that his successive steps toward the acquirement of that home—the gaining of the wealth necessary for its purchase, was like the filling in of the details of the picture, the image of which never faded away from his mind.

And so it if with Financial Success. You must form a mental picture of what you want, and then bend every effort to fill in the picture. Every person should have a purpose in life. To win anything one should have a definite goal for which to strive. We should have a picture in our mind of what we want to own or attain. If we want money, we should create a mental picture of money—we ourselves using it, handling it, spending it, acquiring more, and in short going through all the motions of the man of money. One should paint a great mental picture of wealth, and then start to work to fill in the picture, and to materialize it.

What do you suppose would happen if the architect of the bridge, or building, or the designer of the watch should fail to see in his mind that which he was about to create? Can you not see that there would be no building worthwhile, and that the result of the attempt to build watch, bridge, or skyscraper in this way would result in a mere throwing together of material, without regard to beauty, liability or proper use?

And so it is with the majority of people, they sit down and say "Oh, I want money—I want money," and that is all there is to it. They do not use their imaginations sufficiently to mentally create money, and then proceed to materialize it. They are like a man who would sit down crying out "Oh, I want a wood-pile, high and big with good wood." The man who gets the wood-pile, glances around the place where he wants the pile, and then he forms a mental picture of how that wood-pile will look when completed—just about how high and broad it should be, and then he starts to work to fill in the picture with the wood, working away sawing and piling until at last the picture in materialized.

Oh, I tell you friends, you must first know just what you want, before you will be able to materialize it. Unless you know what you want, you will never get anything. The great successful men of the world have used their imaginations, instead of despising them. They think ahead and create their mental picture, and then go to work materializing that picture in all its details, filling in here, adding a little there, altering this a bit and that a bit, but steadily building—steadily building.

If you would attain Financial Success, you must become a mental creator and designer of that which you long for as well as a material builder. The two go hand in hand and work for Financial Success.

# Concentration

Every person who reads this chapter has heard the word "Concentration" used frequently; has seen it in print often; and has used it repeatedly in conversation. But how few really know just what it means—or are able to form a mental picture of Concentration. Let us consider the term a moment, for until you are able to form a clear mental picture of it, you will not be able to apply it advantageously.

What is "Concentration"? Well, the dictionaries tell us that the word means the act or process of bringing or directing things toward a common center, and thereby condensing and intensifying the force of the thing. And that is the key-note of the word—that is the mental picture of it—this bringing forces to a common center.

One can best form a mental picture of the idea expressed in the word by thinking of a sun-glass which so concentrates the rays of the sun to a focus, or common center, that their powers are intensified upon the spot so that they easily burn a hole through anything placed on the spot.

We can never expect to win out in anything unless we firmly concentrate our minds upon the thing we seek. We have got to make our mental picture of what we want, and then start in to desire it as hard as we are able to, and by so doing we will concentrate our attention and will upon that thing until "something happens." We must learn to concentrate our powers and will upon the desired object, just as the sunglass concentrates the rays of the sun upon the common focus. We must learn to focus our energies upon the thing we want, and then to keep the focus steady from day to day, never allowing ourselves to be side-tracked or swerved from our main object of desire, interest and will.

The majority of people have little or no concentration, and they resemble the puppy-dog whose attention is attracted by first one thing and then another, and who runs from this thing to that, to and fro, not knowing what he wants long enough to get it, but continually wasting his energy in chasing things that have attracted the attention of the moment.

One should begin by practicing concentration on little things, until he masters them, and then he may move on to the consideration and contemplation of larger things. It is quite an art to be able to do one thing at a time, to the exclusion of distracting thoughts and objects. The best workmen along any line of human effort are those who are able to concentrate on their work, and practically lose themselves in their tasks for the time being.

The first step in acquiring Concentration begins, of course, in the control of the attention. Master the attention and you have acquired the art of Concentration. By holding your attention upon a thing, you direct to it your mental forces, and new ideas, plans and combinations spring into your mind and fly to a common center. Besides this you put into operation the Law of Attraction and direct its forces to that same common center. Without concentrated attention yon scatter and dissipate your mental forces and accomplish nothing at all.

I urge upon all who read this book the importance of beginning to cultivate concentration. Begin by acquiring the habit of attending to one thing at a time, concentrating the attention upon it, and then completing it and passing on to another thing. Avoid the baneful practice of thinking of one thing while doing another. Think of and work upon the thing before you, and hold your attention there until it is completed. The thinking and action should pull together, instead of in opposite directions.

An eminent authority tells us that: "It is a matter of no small importance that we acquire the habit of doing only one thing at a time, by which I mean that while attending to any one object, our thoughts ought not to wander to another." Another authority adds: "A frequent cause of failure in the faculty of attention, is striving to think of more than one thing at a time." Another says: "She did things easily because she attended to them in the doing. When she made bread, she thought of bread, and not of the fashion of her next dress, or of her partner at the last dance." The celebrated Lord Chesterfield said: "There is time enough for everything in the course of a day, if you do but one thing at a time; but there is not time enough in a year if you try to do two things at a time."

If then is any secret of concentration, it is contained in the following sentence: You can concentrate on anything you are intensely interested in, or dearly love. For instance, if you are a young man engaged to a beautiful young lady, the ideal woman to make your life complete, you have no trouble in thinking about her and how happy you will be after the knot is tied. In fact, most of your time—when you are not thinking of your work—is given over

to thoughts of that girl, and your future together. Sometimes even her face
pops up before you and you think of her when you should be devoting your
time and thought to the work you are paid for. If you are the proud father of
a new baby girl or boy you have no trouble in thinking about that dear little
bit of humanity. If you are a mother whose son is forging to the front in
business or one of the professions, your thought goes as naturally to that boy
as a duck takes to water. And so we might go down the whole gamut of
humanity and find some one thing which each person is interested in or
loves, and we would soon see that it is not a hard task for a person to think
about or concentrate on that which is most dear to him or her.

Just at the present tune the thing closest to your heart, next, of course, to
that which you actually love, is or should be Financial Independence. For
with money at your disposal you can give that girl everything she needs to
make her happy; you can insure that child's future and make sure that it has
the education which it deserves; you can establish that boy in business and
give him a chance to express his full ability; you can complete those plans you
have had in mind so long and you can do many things which are now
impossible.

It certainly ought not to be hard for you to concentrate on Financial
Independence when it means so much to you, ought it? Well, go to work
now, and when your mind is not occupied with your regular duties, when
your thought is roaming around here and there accomplishing nothing, when
you find yourself thinking of something foolish or vicious, exert your will,
draw back your thought, use your imagination to picture an ideal of what
Financial Independence will mean to you, and then concentrate your whole
thought on that ideal to bring it into materialization. Now is the time to
begin, friend; do not leave it until tomorrow.

# Persistence

In the last chapter we considered the subject of "Concentration," and I tried to show you what an important part it played in the workings of the Law of Financial Success. But, if you concentrate on one thing this minute, and another thing the next moment, and so on, flitting from one flower to another like the butterfly, you will accomplish very little. What is needed is a steady, determined, persistent application to the one object upon which you have set your mind. Having found the object of your desire and knowing how to concentrate upon it, you should then learn how to be Persistent in your concentration, aim, and purpose.

There is nothing like sticking to a thing. Many men are brilliant, resourceful, and industrious, but they fail to reach the goal by reason of their lack of "stick-to-itiveness." One should acquire the tenacity of the bulldog, and refuse to be shaken off of a thing once he has fixed his attention and desire upon it. You remember the old Western hunter who when once he had gazed upon an animal and said "You're my meat," would never leave the trail or pursuit of that animal if he had to track it for weeks, losing his meat in the meantime. Such a man would in time acquire such a faculty of Persistence that the animals would feel like Davy Crockett's coon who cried out; "Don't shoot, mister, I'll come down without it"

You know the dogged persistence inherent in some men that strikes us as an irresistible force when we meet them and come into conflict with their persistent determination. We are apt to call this the "Will," but it is our old friend Persistence— that faculty of holding the Will firmly up against objects, just as the workman holds the chisel against the object on the wheel, never taking off the pressure of the tool until the desired result is obtained.

No matter how strong a Will a man may have, if he has not learned the art of persistent application of it he fails to obtain the best results. One must learn to acquire that constant, unvarying, unrelenting application to the object of his Desire that will enable him to hold his Will firmly against the object until it is shaped according to his wishes. Not only today and tomorrow, but every day until the end.

Burton has said: "The longer I live, the more certain I am that the great difference between men, between the feeble and the powerful, the great and the insignificant, is Energy—Invincible Determination—a purpose once fixed, and then Death or Victory. That quality will do anything that can be done in this world—and no talents, no circumstances, no opportunities, will make a two-legged creature a man without it"

Donald G. Mitchell said: "Resolve is what makes a man manifest; not puny resolve; not crude determinations; not errant purpose—but that strong and indefatigable Will which treads down difficulties and danger, an a boy treads down the heaving frostlands of winter, which kindles his eye and brain with a proud pulse-beat toward the unattainable. Will makes men giants."

Disraeli said: "I have brought myself by long meditation to the conviction that a human being with a settled purpose must accomplish it, and that nothing can resist a Will which will stake even existence upon its fulfillment."

Sir John Simpson said; "A passionate desire, and an unwearied Will can perform impossibilities, or what may seem to be such to the cold and feeble."

And John Foster adds his testimony, when he says: "It is wonderful how even the casualties of life seem to bow to a spirit that will not bow to them, and yield to subserve a design which they may, in their first apparent tendency, threaten to frustrate. When a firm decisive spirit is recognized, it is curious to see how the space clears around a man and leaves him room and freedom."

Abraham Lincoln said of General Grant: "The great thing about him is cool persistency of purpose. He u not easily excited, and he has got the grip of a bull-dog. When he once gets his teeth in, nothing can shake him off."

Now, you may object that the above quotations relate to the Will, rather than to Persistence. But if you stop to consider a moment you will see that they relate to the *persistent* Will, and that the Will without Persistence could accomplish none of these things claimed for it. The Will is the hard chisel, but Persistence is the mechanism that holds the chisel in its place, firmly pressing it up against the object to be shaped, and keeping it from slipping or relaxing its pressure. You cannot closely read the above isolations from these great authorities without feeling a tightness of your lips, and a setting of your jaw, the outward marks of the Persistent Dogged Will.

If you lack Persistence, you should begin to train yourself in the direction of acquiring the habit of sticking to things. This practice will establish a new habit of the mind, and will also tend to cause the appropriate brain-cells to develop and thus give to you as a permanent characteristic the desired quality that you are seeking to develop. Fix your mind upon your daily tasks, studies, occupation or hobbies, and hold your attention firmly upon them by Concentration, until you find yourself getting into the habit of resisting "side-tracking" or distracting influences. It is all a matter of practice and habit. Carry in your mind the idea of the chisel held firmly against the object it is shaping, as given in this chapter—it will help you very much. And read this chapter over and over again, every day or so, until your mind will take up the idea and make it its own. By so doing you will tend to arouse the desire for Persistence and the rest will follow naturally, as the fruit follows the budding and flowering of the tree.

# Habit

Habit is a force which is generally recognized by the average thinking person, but which is commonly viewed in its adverse aspect to the exclusion of its favorable phase. It has been well said that all men are "The creatures of habit," and that "Habit is a cable; we weave a thread of it each day, and it becomes so strong that we cannot break it." But the above quotations only serve to emphasize that side of the question in which men are shown as the slaves of habit, suffering from its confining bonds. There is another side to the question, and that side shall be considered in this chapter.

If it be true that Habit becomes a cruel tyrant ruling and compelling men against their will, desire, and inclination—and this is true in many cases, the question naturally arises in the thinking mind whether this mighty force cannot be harnessed and controlled in the service of man, just as have other forces of Nature. If this result can be accomplished, the man may master Habit and set it to work, instead of being a slave to it and serving it faithfully though complainingly. And the modern psychologists tell us in no uncertain tones that Habit may certainly be thus mastered, harnessed and set to work, instead of being allowed to dominate one's actions and character. And thousands of people have applied this new knowledge and have turned the force of Habit into new channels, and have compelled it to work their machinery of action, instead of being allowed to run to waste, or else permitted to sweep away the structures that men have erected with care and expense, or to destroy fertile mental fields.

A habit is a "mental path" over which our actions have traveled for some time, each passing making the path a little deeper and a little wider. If you have to walk over a field or through a forest, you know how natural it is for you to choose the clearest path in preference to the less worn ones, and greatly in preference to stepping out across the field or through the woods and making a new path. And the line of mental action is precisely the same. It in movement along the lines of the least resistance— passage over the well-worn path. Habits are created by repetition and are formed in accordance to a natural law, observable in all animate things and some would say in inanimate things as well. As an instance of the latter, it is pointed out that a piece of paper once folded in a certain manner will fold along the same lines the next time. And all users of sewing machines, or other delicate pieces of mechanism, know that as a machine or instrument is once "broken in" so will it tend to run thereafter. The same law is also observable in the ruse of musical instruments. Clothing or gloves form into creases according to the person using them, and these creases once formed will always be in effect, notwithstanding repeated pressings. Rivers and streams of water cut their courses through the land, and thereafter flow along the habit-course. The law is in operation everywhere.

The above illustrations will help you to form the idea of the nature of habit, and will aid you in forming new mental paths—new mental creases. And, remember this always—the best (and one might say the only) way in which old habits may be removed is to form new habits to counteract and replace the old undesirable ones. Form new mental paths over which to travel, and the old ones will soon become less distinct and in time will practically fill up from disuse. Every time you travel over the path of the desirable mental habit, you make the path deeper and wider, and make it so much easier to travel it thereafter. This mental path-making is a very important thing, and I cannot urge upon you too strongly the injunction to start to work making the desirable mental paths over which you wish to travel. Practice, practice, practice—be a good path-maker.

The following rules will help you in your work in forming new habits:

1. At the beginning of the formation of a new habit, put force into your expression of the action, thought, or characteristic. Remember that you are taking the first steps toward making the new mental path, and it is much harder at the first than it will be afterwards. Make the path as clear and deep as you can, at the start, so that you can see it readily the next time you wish to travel it.

2. Keep your attention firmly concentrated on the new path building, and keep your eyes and thoughts away from the old paths, lest you incline toward them. Forget all about the old paths, and concern yourself only with the new one that you are building.

3. Travel over your newly made path as often as possible. Make opportunities for doing so, without waiting for them to arise. The oftener you go over the new path, the sooner will it become an old, well-worn, easily traveled one. Think out plans for passing over it and using it, at the start.

4. Resist the temptation to travel over the older easier paths that you have been using in the past. Every time you resist a temptation, the stronger do you become, and the easier will it be for you to do so the next time. But every time you yield to the temptation, the easier does it become to yield again, and the more difficult does it become to resist the next time. You will have a fight on at the start, and this is the critical time. Prove your determination, persistency, and Will power now, right here at the start.

5. Be sure that you have mapped out the proper path—plan it out well, and see where it will lead you to—then go ahead without fear and without allowing yourself to doubt. "Place your hand upon the plow, and look not backward" Your goal is Financial Success—then make a good, deep, wide mental path leading straight to it.

# Claiming Your Own

There has grown up in the minds of many people the delusion that there is some real merit in taking the mental position that desirable things are "too good for me," and denying that they have any merit whatsoever in them. So prevalent has become this idea that it has developed a race of hypocrites and pharisees, who go about proclaiming their humble goodness, and their meek humility, until one gets tired of hearing their talk—and talk is all there is to it, for these same people slyly manage to reach out for the good things in sight, even while decrying the value of the aforesaid good things, and denying their worthiness to receive anything at all.

I take quite the other position. I believe that there is nothing too good for the men and women who assert their right to live and to partake of the good things of earth. I am reminded of the French soldier who carried a dispatch to Napoleon, and whose horse dropped dead from fatigue as he sprang from it and handed the Emperor the dispatch which he had carried from miles away. Napoleon wrote an answer, and dismounting from his horse handed the bridle to the soldier, saying "Take this horse and ride back, comrade." "Nay," cried the soldier as he gazed at the blooded horse and his trappings, "it is too magnificent and grand for me, a common soldier." "Take it!" cried Napoleon, "there is nothing too grand and magnificent for a soldier of France!" And these words, rapidly repeated through the ranks and columns of his army, gave to his tired troops a new and fresh inspiration and energy. "Nothing too grand and magnificent for a soldier of France," they said, and the thought that they were such worthy individuals inspired them to the almost miraculous deeds that followed.

Napoleon understood human nature, and the laws of psychology. Tell a man that he is a worm of the dust, and deserving of nothing but kicks and punishment, and if he believes you he will sink to the mental level of the worm and will cringe and crawl and eat dirt. But let him know that he has within him the divine spark, and that there is nothing too good for him; nothing that he has not a right to aspire to; no heights which are not his own if he but climb to them—tell him these things, I say, and he will become a transfigured creature, ready and willing to attempt great things, and do mighty deeds, "As a man thinketh in his heart, so is he."

And that is why I am trying to tell you that you have a right to all the good things there are—that you are a worthy human being and not a crawling thing of the dust. That is why I tell you to raise up your head and look the world in the eyes, affirming your relationship with the Divine Cause that brought you into being, and asserting your right to partake of your heritage from that Power.

Does not all Nature seem to come to the aid and assistance of the strong individuals who assert their right to live, and prosper? Does not Nature seem to try in every way to build up strong, confident, self-reliant, self-respecting individuals? Does it not seem to reserve the prizes of life for the strong hand that has courage to reach out and take them, instead of to those cringing, shrinking personalities that cower and shiver back in the corner, afraid to call their souls their own?

There is nothing in Nature that gives any encouragement whatsoever to this false teaching of mock humility, and self-abasement of which we hear so much. The very persons who hold up this weak, negative ideal to their followers, are not especially noted for their meekness or humility—they are apt to be arrogant, selfish and grasping all the good things in sight, even while decrying and denying them. They are all words, words, words, with their cant phrases and negative admonitions. Away with such destructive and hurtful teachings. Make way for the new teaching that the good things of earth have been placed here for man's use, and for his development and happiness. There is nothing too good for Men or Women, for they are the rightful inheritors and heirs of their Divine Causer.

Does not Nature seem to strive to produce strong plants, strong animals, strong individuals? Does she not seem to delight in producing an individual, in either of the great kingdoms of life, who has the desire, energy, ambition and power to draw to itself the nourishment and nutriment which will enable it to express its life fully— which will enable it to become a proper, efficient and worthy channel through which may flow the great Stream of Life that has its source in the Divine Cause which is behind and back of all things? Is life but an effort to produce weak, miserable, unhappy beings—or is it an urge that seeks to develop strong, happy, noble individual forms? And how can one be happy, strong, and noble if the source of supply is denied him? What would the plant become if its nourishment were withdrawn?

And yet in spite of all these apparent facts of Nature, there are those who would have us refuse the full supply which the Divine Power has placed at our hand and bidden us partake thereof. These people would even deny the supply. Oh, I say to you, friends, the Power that called us into being has placed in this world of ours all that is necessary to our well-being, and has implanted in our breasts the natural hunger for nourishment, physical, mental and spiritual. This very hunger is Nature's promise that there exists that which is intended to satisfy it. And then, what folly to decry the hunger, or to deny the supply. That which you need and for which you are hungry, exists for you. It is yours, and you are not robbing others when you seek for it and draw it to you.

Claim Your Own, friends, Claim Your Own! Deny it not—decry it not—but cry aloud "It is Mine Own—I Demand It—I attract it to Me!" Claim Your Own!

# Making Money

"The possession of money gives confidence, the lack of it self-consciousness."

IN the preceding chapters of this book we have discussed "The Law of Financial Success," and suggested methods and given instruction for the development of the various positive qualities necessary to the one who desires to get into harmony with the *Law*.

But our exposition of the *Law* is not yet complete. Like everything else in Nature, it has two sides: for instance, we have male and female, heat and cold, light and darkness, sunshine and rain, and one is just as necessary to the whole as is the other.

We have said very little as to the handling of money. What has gone before was extremely practical and all very necessary, because we must "know" before we "do"—we must "possess" before we "use." If you have read carefully and studied with a purpose that which has preceded, and have decided to take advantage of the suggestions given, you are now ready for this final chapter, "Making Money," toward which all the others have been leading you.

A person might possess every one of the positive qualities, but if he were in the back woods or the Desert of Sahara, where there is no money in circulation, he never could become financially independent, for the second part of the *Law* could not be brought into action. And again, on the other hand, a person might be left a mint of money and if he did not know how to take care of it, or if he did not possess the necessary positive qualities by means of which he might make more money, he would lose it all in a few years, and he himself become a tramp of the worst type. This is not an uncommon occurrence, and may be verified at any shelter house or Salvation Army Barracks in our larger cities.

An illustration from real life, showing how the *Law* worked in one instance will here be given. The writer is acquainted with a gentleman of middle age now occupying an enviable position in financial circles, and when, because of the development of the positive qualities, will before he dies become much more prominent and leave his mark on the world. This man was born "with a gold spoon in his mouth," and all during his youthful days had everything and anything a young man could want, as well as many things he did not need. In time reverses came, and these, combined with extravagance, swept away the fortune that had been bequeathed to him.

Here was a young man about twenty years of age left without a dollar, and with absolutely no training in the direction of earning a living. After a few years of the hardest kind of knocks, he made his way to the far West. There he obtained an inside position where he worked for a time, until it began to tell on his health. One day while at work in the office, and wondering what was going to become of him, a great truth dawned on his mind. It was this: I can never amount to anything or become very wealthy like my father by merely working with my hands. The only way to make money is to compel money to work for me.

With a definite object in view, he gave up his inside "position" and took a "job" on the railroad grade as a teamster. In less than six months, by depriving himself of every luxury, he had accumulated enough money to partly pay for one pair of mules. These he hired out, acting himself as driver. After a while he bought a second pair on credit, giving a mortgage on both pair for payment, and hired a man to drive the second pair. When that pair was paid for he bought two more pairs, again mortgaging all he had to pay for the second two pairs. When they were paid for he bought four more pairs, and then he went to work, not as a hired man, but as a contractor on his own account in a small way, and thus made money. The capital invested in these mules worked for him, and step by step in a few years he was in a position of affluence and power.

This man, just like every other man, had the germs of the positive qualities in him. All they needed was developing. This development was obtained by the knocks he received, both before and after that great truth dawned upon him.

Let me again express that truth in a little different language so that it may be impressed upon the mind of every one of my readers: No man ever became very wealthy working with his hands alone; this applies to the brain worker also. The only way to obtain much money is to make money work for you.

Jay Gould, the noted financier, once said: "One hundred dollars invested in the right place at the right time will earn as much as one man steadily employed." This is a great truth too, in financial matters, that we must let sink deeply into our consciousness.

But the question right now with many is, "How shall we acquire the first one hundred dollars so as to invest it?" And the only answer is, by saving it. There is no person, who, if he can earn wages, but can in time, by sacrificing some luxury, or by rigid economy, lay aside one, two or three hundred dollars. And the best way to do this is by putting in some good savings bank a stated sum each week, no matter how small that sum may be. One of the best aids to this is the metal bank in which you can drop your odd change, such as are loaned to their customers by up-to-date savings institutions. If you keep this up long enough, you are bound to acquire your first hundred dollars. By doing this you have acquired at the same time two valuable habits—economy and patience.

It is now necessary to place or invest this money, and more to be obtained in like manner, where it will bring back to you the largest possible returns and yet be perfectly safe. And the question comes to one at this point, "Shall I go into business for myself, as the young man did, or shall I work for another and invest my savings and watch them grow?"

That depends. If you have developed the qualities of courage, initiative, self-confidence and grit to a remarkable degree, and the opportunity presents itself, go into business for yourself and you will win. If not, hold onto your present position, but be always on the lookout to better yourself, and increase your salary, and in the meantime invest your surplus money in some good security.

When making an investment do not be blinded either by your own prejudice or the prejudice or craftiness of some stock, bond, mortgage or banking house salesman. Remember this—and in doing so realize that it is a frailty of human nature and the instinct of self-preservation that makes it so—that whatever a man or firm is offering for sale at the time you approach them is the best thing for you to buy. Other investments offered by other firms may be good—but, this is best for you. Realize this frailty, use your own judgment, don't knock the other fellow, and invest in what seems best to you after hearing the stories of all of them.

The writer can command no language strong enough in which to express his contempt for the social parasite who obtains the money of people under false pretenses or by making glittering promises of great wealth on short notice without ever intending or expecting to make any returns. It matters not whether he be an absconding cashier or president of a bank, the president or representative of a noted stock or bond house, who has knowingly sold the stocks or bonds of a corporation that is watered beyond all limits, or a "fake" mining promoter. These men all belong in the same class, they are rascals and their place is behind the prison bars.

I shall now present, as concisely as possible, the various methods of investing money, and in an unprejudiced manner give the advantages and disadvantages of each.

At the head of all investments, as regards safety of capital, stand government bonds. They are in no way attractive to the small investor, because of the low rate of interest. Their principal demand is by National Banks, which are compelled to buy and deposit these bonds with the United States Treasurer, to protect their issue of bank bills. State bonds are considered almost as safe as government bonds (though some states have repudiated their obligations), but also pay a low rate of interest.

Savings banks pay their depositors three and sometimes four percent. Placing money in a savings bank may be regarded as an investment, since the depositor loans his money to the banker, and he in turn uses that money to earn money for the stockholders of the bank. It would take a great many years for a man to acquire a competence or to become financially independent by merely keeping his money in a savings bank.

Municipal bonds, including county, city, town, school, water, city hall, sewer and special assessment bonds pay from four to five percent. The best ones are in large demand, at these low rates of interest, by large estates and trustees for the investment of trust funds, the investing of which is restricted by law to securities of this character. Some municipal bonds are safer than others, depending upon the standing and character of the municipality issuing them. All depend upon some form of taxation for the payment of interest, as well as principal. The best way to purchase municipal bonds is to get in touch with some reputable bond house making a specialty of them, and buy under the instruction of some man whom you can trust to tell the truth.

Steam and electric railway bonds and public service corporation bonds may all be classed together for convenience sake. They pay from four to seven percent. In buying them it is best to consult an authority, as some are very much safer than others.

Real estate mortgages pay from four to eight percent, depending upon locality and the character of security, and are in large demand by a class of investors who have sums varying from $5,000 and upwards, and who depend upon this class of investment for an income. In buying real estate mortgages, know the people who are placing the mortgages—their ability to make the interest payments, and whether there is any chance of default. There is a moral as well as a financial obligation involved here.

Real estate pays anywhere from five to ten percent, depending upon its location. While there are opportunities for large profits in the appreciation of real estate in some localities, there is always the risk of great depreciation. One thing should be remembered in buying real estate for a permanent investment and that is the danger of booms, with their enthusiasm, lack of judgment, inflated prices and general lack of conservatism. Remember that the yield should be adequate to the risk—see to it that the uncertainty of an income is reduced to a minimum.

Industrial stocks pay from five to twenty percent, and are dependent largely upon the commercial conditions of the country, the nature of the business, the amount of competition, and the character of the management. The utmost caution should be exercised in investing your savings in stocks of this character, and you must know absolutely that you are dealing with reliable, capable and honest people.

The stocks of legitimate mining companies pay from six to many hundred percent on the par value, and are dependent upon the diameter and location of the property, and the reliability of the men in control. There is always great danger to the small investor in putting his money into mining stocks, as he is not in a position to determine, as a rule, the intrinsic value of same. He must depend wholly upon the character and reliability of the men who are responsible for the intelligent and conscientious use of his money in the operation of a mining property. More fortunes have been made in mining than in any other of the many industries in the United States. There have also been many a poor man's and woman's hard earned savings lost by turning over their little all to some glib-tongued promoter while there was not at any time even a remote possibility of ever getting any return.

The all-important question, when investing your money, is to know those with whom you are doing business. There are many meritorious propositions being handled by honest, capable men, which offer great opportunities to the small investor, and if he can but use careful judgment and discretion in determining the right persons to do business with, there is no reason why the most humble cannot acquire a competency by careful and intelligent investing.

The reader may know of or learn about lots of other ways of investing money, besides those presented above. If so, and they "look good to you" after putting the facts in each case through the mill of Reason and Judgment, take advantage of the opportunity. If you lose, do not be a "namby-pamby" and cry over spilt milk; "get busy" and begin again.

And even if great reverses come and everything you possess is swept away, don't sink back in despair and give up the ship. Rest a while and then go at it again harder than ever, but this time follow the *Law*. It is no sin to go broke or even to be bankrupt. The dishonor lies in remaining so. As Josh Billings said: "Sukces don't konsist in never makin' mistakes, but in never makin' the same one twice." And Ella Wheeler Wilcox writes:

"Tis easy enough to be pleasant
When life flows by like a song,
But the man worth while Is the man with a smile
When everything goes dead wrong."

In judging any investment it is always wise to know a few inside facts in regard to the proposition offered. The only way to find out anything is by asking questions either of yourself, while you are reading the "prospectus," or else of the officers of the company, if you do not find these questions answered somewhere in the literature.

The following "Investors' Questions" are taken from a book called "Financing an Enterprise" by Francis Cooper, published by the Ronald Press, and will bring out the truth in regard to an investment, if anything will. Don't hesitate to ask them of anyone who wants you to invest your money with him.

I. NATURE OF ENTERPRISE.
1. Is the basis of the enterprise sound?
2. Is the business or undertaking profitable elsewhere?
3. What competition or opposition will be met?
4. What peculiar advantages does it enjoy over these others?
5. Can it be conducted profitably under existing conditions?

II. PLAN OF ORGANIZATION
1. In what state organized?
2. What is the capitalization?
3. Is the capitalization reasonable?
4. Has the stock been issued in whole or in part and if so what?
5. Is the stock offered for sale full-paid and non-assessable?
6. Has any of the stuck preferences?
7. Is any stock unissued or held in the treasury?
8. Who has stock control?
9. Are the rights of smaller stockholders protected?
10. Are there any unusual features in charter or by-laws?

## III. PRESENT CONDITION OF ENTERPRISE

As to Property.

1. What properties or rights are controlled?

2. What is their value and how estimated?

3. Are these properties or rights owned, or held under lease, license, grant, option or otherwise?

4. If owned, are titles perfect?

5. Are there any encumbrances on the properties or rights?

6. If not owned, are the holding papers in due form?

7. If not owned, are the terms of building reasonable, satisfactory and safe?

8. In event of liquidation, what would be worth of property?

As to Operation.

1. What operations have been or are now carried on?

2. What have been the results?

3. What difficulties, if any, have been encountered?

4. What is the demand for the product or operation of the enterprise?

5. What is present status of the enterprise?

6. Are proper books kept?

As to Finance.

1. What are the present assets and their actual value?

2. What debts, claims, fees, rents, royalties or other payments or obligations are now due or are to be met and carried?

3. From what resources are these to be met?

4. Who handles the moneys and under what safeguards?

5. What are or will be the running expenses, salaries, etc.?

## IV. MANAGEMENT.

Directors.

1. How many members in the board?

2. Who are these members?

3. What is their past record and present business status?

4. Who are the active members of the board?

5. Who, if any, are inactive?

6. Are meetings regularly held and attended?

7. Who compose the executive committee, if any, and what are its powers?

8. Are the directors stockholders to a material

Officers.

1. Who we the officers?

2. What are their previous records?

3. What are their special present qualifications?

4. Are they able to work together without friction?

5. What compensation do they receive or are they to receive?

6. Are they interested in the enterprise beyond their salaries?

## V. PLAN OF OPERATION.

1. What is the general plan of operation?

2. What special reasons, if any, led to its adoption?

## VI. THE PROPOSITION.

1. Is the general proposition a fair one?

2. Is the price of .stock or bonds reasonable?

3. How do these prices compare with any former prices?

4. If common stock is offered, do preferred stock, bonds or other profit-sharing obligations take precedence and to what amount?

5. What reserve of profits will be retained before dividends are to be declared?

6. If preferred stock is offered, is it cumulative, does it vote, when is it redeemable and at what price, what sinking fund provision is made for redemption and are any peculiar provisions attached? Do any bonds or other obligations take precedence of the preferred stock?

7. If bonds are offered, what interest is paid, and when and where; upon what property are they secured, and when and how paid; is the trustee or trust company of repute; under what conditions are the bonds foreclosable; when and how are they or may they be redeemed; are there any other securities taking precedence, and are there any peculiar provisions in deed of trust?

## VII. GENERAL.

1. What u the previous history of the enterprise or the property or undertaking on which it is based?

2. If inventions enter prominently, what is the previous record of the inventor?

3. By whom are the statements made, and is the party making them reliable?

4. Are there any contracts or obligations, not now effective, by which the enterprise will subsequently be affected?

www.ingramcontent.com/pod-product-compliance
Lightning Source LLC
Chambersburg PA
CBHW021913040426
42447CB00007B/829